Copyright © 2015 by Deidré L. Pratt. All rights reserved. This book or any portion thereof may not be reproduced or used in any manner whatsoever without the express written permission of the publisher except for the use of brief quotations in a book review.

My Worth Ministries, Inc., Snellville, Georgia
Printed in the United States of America

ISBN 978-0-692-32929-0

www.myworthministries.com

...an inspiring anthology of pearls of wisdom,
celebrating the value of women across generations

By

Deidré Pratt

A publication of My Worth Ministries, Inc.

Table of Contents

Introduction	Deidré Pratt	3
I Know My Worth	Sandra Allen, Esq.	5
Healing from the Inside Out	Kay Bell	7
A Dancer's Prayer	Olivia Bennett	9
Discovering Your Worth, Unearthing Your Value	Doreen Priscilla Brown	11
African American Woman	O. Lisa Dabreu, Esq.	13
A Song in My Heart, a Melody in My Spirit	Rachel Dabreu	15
A Priceless Child	Toussaint Duchess-Campbell	17
The Words That Matter Most	Dana Evans, Ph.D.	19
The Birth of Worth!	Regina Gibbs, D. D.	21
Young Believer: Growing in My Worth	India Hunt	23
From Africa to America	Caroline Kelly	25
My Alabaster Box	Gwendolyn Knight	27
The Joys Motherhood	Deidré Pratt & Cameron Sample	29
Let the Circle Be Unbroken	Deidré Pratt	31
Tender Seedlings of Worth	Zaria Davis, Ava Prince, Tia Williams	33
There is No Rainbow Without a Little Rain	Grace Lee	35
Marana tha: Come, O Lord	Yoon Pender	37
In the Garden	Deidré Pratt	39
God's Promise	Alexis Prince	41
A Journey of Trust	Adia Randall	43
From Broadway to the Bible	Daryl Richardson	45
Beautiful. Brilliant. Magnificent You!	Kinnik Sky	47
Broken, but Not Destroyed	Gayle Stallworth	49
From the Army to God's Soldier	Sonja Stribling	51
Walking by Faith	Stacey Uche	53
Strength, Worth and Joy are in His Dwelling Place	Diana Wagner	55
Breaking the Silence of Child Sexual Abuse	Angela Williams	57
Healing Hands	Brittany Williams, D.C.	59
I Choose—a poem	Deidré Pratt	61
Epilogue	Deidré Pratt	62
WORTH Emerging Women Leaders STEM Scholarship Award	Deidré Pratt	63
Acknowledgements and Credits	Deidré Pratt	64

Introduction

Worth. Matter. Live.

When a woman knows her worth, her life is forever changed. She lives.

When a woman embraces her worth, she knows she matters. She lives intentionally, daily. She pursues a life of significance that has little to do with career, fame, or fortune and everything to do with her influence—an eternal influence that lives beyond her. It's her desire and resolve to make her todays and tomorrows better. It begins in the recesses of her heart, and manifests itself from the center of that divine and sacred place.

When a woman understands her worth, she is not misguided about who she is. She does not compromise her values. She does not repeat poor decisions. And, she does not require others to validate her, or grant her permission to live out her dreams and God's vision for her life. She moves forward in confidence . . . in excellence. The world notices her—in every setting, in each situation.

Worth. Self-worth asks: *How valuable am I?*

My Worth Ministries, Inc. empowers young girls and women to address the question of self-worth. Within the pages of *Worth*, you'll discover women across generations who have grown in spirit to confidently answer this question with courage and conviction.

Worth is an inspiring journey, unfolding the richness and beauty of the lives of our mothers, daughters, sisters, wives and friends. We invite you to join us on this journey of life and living. Listen to their heartfelt stories. Hear how they've overcome their fears, doubts and insecurities. And, learn how they've come to embrace remarkable and fruitful lives of value and self-worth.

We know when our young girls and women are better, our sons and brothers are better. When our sons and brothers are better, our husbands and families are better. And, when our families are better, our communities flourish and sustain as the fabric of a healthy society and the world at large!

Worth keeps on giving. Worth keeps on living. Worth keeps on . . . .

I Know My Worth

Sandra Allen
Author and Attorney

Before I came to Christ, I was on a mission to become rich and successful. Materialistic and self-centered, I spent most of my time working, shopping and partying. Life was going from one "good time" to the next, with little concern for the misery of others.

Raised by my parents to be nice and go to school, I completed college and law school, passed the bar exam, and began work as a prosecutor. I absolutely hated it. After eleven long months, I quit and began working at another legal job, which I also disliked. I continued practicing law because I wanted the money and liked the lifestyle, but it left me feeling bored and empty.

After several years of chasing the brass ring and finally "arriving," I was bored out of my mind. I quit job after job until one day I was contacted by a legal recruiter for an interview. During the interview, she invited me to a Bible study. Once there, I had an encounter with God that changed my life. After attending for a while, I became filled with the Holy Spirit and power. I began to seek God with a fervency and an urgency that completely consumed me. As a result, most of my friends bailed on me and, eventually, so did my husband. Others told me I was crazy, but I knew different. God was doing a work; and I was the work in progress.

No longer was I ruled by how much money I made, I was led by the Lord. As I walked with God and trusted Him, I learned that in Him I cannot fail. I learned my true worth—that I am priceless, a rare jewel, the apple of His eye. Free from the influences that are not of God, I learned I had to be my absolute best to glorify His name. God has called me to be a prophetic voice and a giver in His kingdom. So, I desire to be a channel of blessing to those around me, to those He brings near and to those who cross my path. I belong to Him.

My best advice: Follow your heart. Follow your instincts—no matter the situation, no matter the circumstance. God will provide if you don't have the resources, and He will bring others to help if you are all alone. Don't dim your light for the comfort of others. Sidestep those who simply cannot bear your blessing. Don't allow fear to hinder you. Fear is a dream killer and is not of God.

I wrote *The Anointing of the Queen* as an expression of my life, to see women transformed and to address the subliminal messages in society that demean the value of women. Women are viewed as sex objects, face discrimination in the workplace, and suffer age-old traditions of what we can and cannot do. If we embrace the notion that women are "less than," we believe a lie and become stagnant. God's Word proclaims there is neither male nor female in Christ Jesus, and His Word is truth.

To whom much is given, much is required. I feel blessed to have had many opportunities to become educated, travel, write books, meet people of all ethnicities and cultures, and speak to women about their worth and potential as well as discover my own. My intention is to die "empty"—to pour out every gift and talent, develop every idea and inspiration, and to continually reinvent myself in every season of my life. I love being a woman. I love that I am free to be me. I am priceless. I am made in God's image. There is absolutely no one like me.

Healing from the Inside Out

Kay Bell
Business Owner

As my husband Andy and I left the doctor's office in 2012, I felt I'd been given a death sentence. The doctor assured us that the only viable cure for my arterial blockage was the same surgery my grandfather had before his stroke, and that the procedure had since been perfected. But had it really? The memories of my grandfather's debility and years of suffering until his death flashed through my mind. At age 57, I wouldn't concede without a fight.

Daily I searched the web for answers, and many links led me to new studies on the American diet and its devastating effect on our health. I discovered there were options, if I was willing to change my diet completely. The studies I read pointed to reversals of more serious cases than mine. A plant-based, no-oil-added diet would be extreme, but certainly worth the effort. When Andy said we would do it together, the necessary change seemed attainable.

As we worked through this health crisis we began the process of relocating from our home of 30 years to our new home, requiring our leaving friends and neighbors we loved. As my life changed I prayed for new friends, a new career direction and improved health, and slowly I began to see God at work all around me. Little did I know how God would use my health issues to answer many of the prayer requests I had laid before Him.

After seven months on the diet, tests revealed that my arteries were clear and my blood pressure and cholesterol in normal ranges. The good news didn't stop there—pain in my joints from a previous injury was gone, pounds dropped off—and not just for me, but for Andy, too. Was changing our diet easy? Absolutely not. But, was it worth it? Absolutely yes! Along the way God reminded me that we are created in His image and are the temples where the Holy Spirit dwells. It matters to Him what we do with our bodies. Timothy 1:7 says: "God didn't give us a spirit of timidity, but a spirit of power and love and self-discipline." He wants us to exercise self-discipline in all things, and if we aren't healthy how can we be His hands to minister to others?

As we changed our lifestyle, God combined my prayers for friends and career re-direction with a "chance meeting" with a regional vice-president of a company that markets health, beauty, and personal care products. She invited me to her home and shared first that the company's product line was unparalleled in quality and value and then, next, explained the potential of the business opportunity. At that meeting I sensed that God's redeeming power was at work just as He promises in Romans 8:28 that He "causes all things to work together for good to those who love (Him) . . ."

Today, as an independent consultant with this company, I see God's blessings as I work alongside new friends, sharing with others what I've learned about health and introducing them to products that are pure, safe, and beneficial. But most importantly, I've learned that God hears and answers prayers in His own time and in His own way. And, I've watched with deep gratitude as He worked in ways that were beyond what I could even imagine.

"For I know the plans I have for you," declares the Lord, "plans to prosper you and not to harm you, plans to give you hope and a future."

– Jeremiah 29:11

A Dancer's Prayer

Olivia Bennett
Elementary School Student
and Ballerina

Lord, thank you for blessing me to dance wonderfully. When I spin, it makes me feel like you are lifting me away. When I jump in the air, I feel like an angel with wings to fly. Dancing is an awesome feeling. It makes me feel like I am accomplishing something as you have given me a great skill. God, you have designed my body perfectly to dance. I feel very confident when I stand with poise. Thank you for standing there with me.

You allow me to remember all the routines in my head. Thank you for giving me the brilliance to remember all the moves, especially in the jazz waltz. Doing the jazz waltz, I walk to my side and shake my hips at the same time. This takes a lot of coordination, and you've made me great at it. You've given me grace and style.

I move my long and slender arms gracefully as my dance teacher instructs me to. I am a ballerina. I move my arms even faster when I want to make the beat and rhythm move through my body. That's how excited I get when I feel your presence. My legs are long and strong because they do more work than the rest of my body. I strengthen my legs even more by taking swimming classes. I do this because I want to take care of my body so I can be the best dancer and use the gift you have given me. I want to make you proud.

There are times I have to stand up really tall on my tippy-toes and spin around without losing my balance. It is the strength of my legs that helps me not to fall. Thank you for strengthening me. I have to smile all the time when I perform, so when the audience sees me they know I am happy about what I do. When I dance, I want them to know I love what I do and that I do my very best to get to the top. My smile shines brightly because I know it's a reflection of your glory in me to others. When the audience claps for me, it makes me feel happy. I am especially happy when I see my parents and my sisters sit there in the crowd and cheer for me.

God, I hear you whisper to me that I am doing very well and that the angels are all around me. Jesus, thank you for my friends who also dance with me. I encourage them to work very hard and to pray so you can help them as they dance and also help them remember their routines, because this is what I do.

And, thank you for Cameron, an older dancer on another team who wins a lot of competitions. She inspires me. She dances really well too, and she always has her routines figured out. She helps me out sometimes, and I pray that you bless her for that.

Jesus, thank you for allowing me to believe in myself because I try to do my best in everything. My mommy tells me to follow my dreams because I am worth it. I thank you, Lord, for this amazing gift you have given me to be a good dancer and a great ballerina. Amen!

Discovering Your Worth, Unearthing Your Value

Doreen Priscilla Brown
Author and Adjunct Professor

It's amazing how God can move you from one degree of grace to another when you fully trust Him. And, it is in trusting Him, and yielding to the Holy Spirit, you can truly find your worth. The fact is there is no mountain high enough and no valley low enough where God cannot ascend or descend in order to speak to you so that you can hear His voice and be motivated to move toward all He has in store for you. For our God is an ever-present God—a trustworthy confidant, a teller of truth, and a voice of reason at times of trial and tribulation.

The late Maya Angelou once reminded participants at a forum to not ever "adjust your price tag," which made me look at my own worth in a completely different light. It is true that we so often settle for a little because we feel a little something is more than nothing. But, may I remind you that this is a lie from the pit of hell. If you believe the only fruit you can reach is the low hanging one, then you will never aspire to climb that ladder to capture the unspoiled fruit, basking in the sun, still rich and firm with its nutrients intact.

That being said, why is it important to discover your worth? Why is it important to buy into David's admonishment to wait on the Lord? Listen to him in Psalm 27:14: "Wait for the Lord; be strong and take heart and wait for the Lord." I encourage you to take heed to David's sage advice, as the virtue of patience in waiting on the Lord will, assuredly, lead you to discover your worth, unearth your value.

God is saying to each seeker, first, EVALUATE YOURSELF. See if you are in right-standing before God. There is no need to put yourself into a torture chamber—just evaluate yourself introspectively, knowing that God will keep your secret!

If you are, like me, among the more mature women whom God has blessed with another lease on life, no worries. Though you may have missed the chance to get your "sheet stuff" right the first time around, there is no need to panic—my God is a big God, a forgiving God. Although others may deliberately ignore their own bloopers and criticize your "sheet" decisions, you can be personally confident in your belief that there is a God of second chances . . . a God who rolls up beside you and provides you with affirmation at times when your cup of self-doubt may be filled to the brim.

Keep this truth close to your breast: Being pure does not necessarily mean you cannot reclaim your honor after a mess-up. Know this—you absolutely can experience a do-over from the point of your slip-up; for the matter of purity is not just of a sexual nature, but more so it is a spiritual attitude and a heart for a compassionate God who " . . . has called you out of darkness into His wonderful light" (1 Peter 2:9).

Congratulations, Deidré Lynette Pratt for your vision for women! You may not know it now, but you stand on the cusp of a breakthrough. So many women, young and older, are yearning to be part of a ministry such as My Worth Ministries, where they can feel, touch and experience the fullness of joy in their lives—no matter how fractured or broken they may be at the moment!

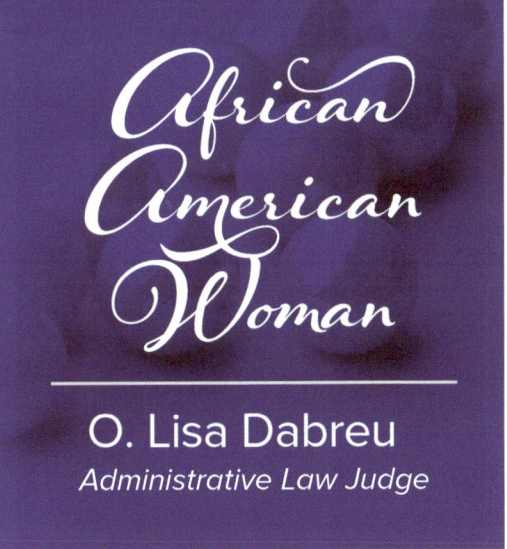

African American Woman

O. Lisa Dabreu
Administrative Law Judge

How can I call myself African?
For my feet have never touched your dark rich earth.
My eyes have never gazed upon the sun rising on your beautiful green lands
Or the moon's reflections against your radiant blue waters.

How can I call myself African?
It's because my heart can feel the wounds and pain of my great-great grandparents, as they were torn away from their homeland.
And because I have heard about the vision of my great-great grandmother, a slave, as she stood in a field, crying out, "Lord give this land to my children's children."
I pray that this vision stays before me, for encouragement, as I reach "toward the mark for the prize of the high calling of God."

How can I call myself African?
It's because of the color of my skin that is of the earth from which God created me.
Because my countenance is strong, my nose is prominent, and my heart is filled with His love.
Because my dark eyes sparkle, as the stars that God placed in the heavens.
Because my lips are pleasantly full, and I pray that they shall always speak words of wisdom and of love from God's own heart.
Because my head is lifted up, not with pride, but so that my eyes are forever focused on my Saviour.

How can I call myself American?
It's because of the blood shed by my ancestors on American soil as they fought, first, for the freedom of this country and, then, for their very own freedom within this country.
Because of my prayers that people of all races love one another, as God has commanded.

How can I call myself American?
It's because I am proud that this country was founded by faithful men and women who revered God, and whose lives evidenced perseverance and obedience to His calling.
Because I pray that my steps shall likewise be ordered by God and that I shall live my life in a manner pleasing to Him.
And because of the hope that I have that my son's steps also shall be ordered by God, and that he shall be one of America's great leaders of the future, testifying of God's love and fulfilling His precepts.

How can I call myself American?
It's because I am committed to fulfilling God's ordained purpose for me in America and across this land.
Because I desire to see this country rise up and lead the world by living out the true meaning of the moral creed that this nation was "conceived in liberty and dedicated to the proposition that all men are created equal."
Yes, I think that I shall call myself an African American woman, consecrated to God.

Copyright Registration Number: TXu 845-911

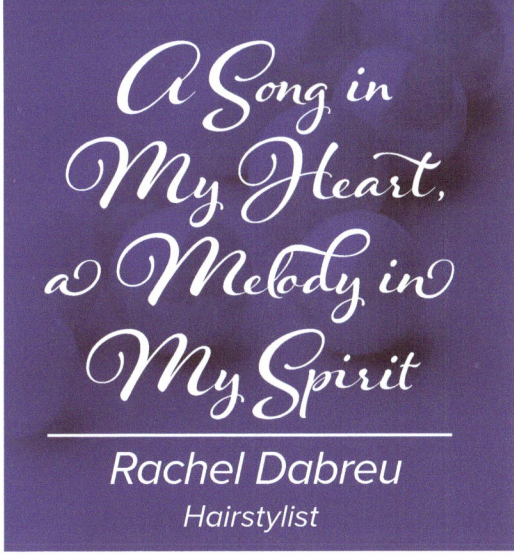

A Song in My Heart, a Melody in My Spirit

Rachel Dabreu
Hairstylist

This is the only song I have ever written that has been put to music and actually sung by someone other than me. (I don't usually write songs.) I have always had a love of worshiping God through music. My mom tells a story of me singing "O Victory in Jesus" at the top of my lungs as she pushed me through the grocery store in a shopping cart.

I have been a worship leader throughout many phases of my life—in youth group, in college, and as a missionary in the Netherlands. It was during my time in the Netherlands that I wrote the lyrics to this song—lyrics that truly express my heart for the Lord and the Lord's heart for us.

Many years after I wrote these lyrics, I experienced the deeper truth behind them as I struggled through a rough time in my life. I definitely had lost my way and the Lord's love guided me back. Darkness clouded my life, but the Lord was faithful in shining His light and helping me see His truth in the midst of my struggle. My heart was broken and God's comfort, through the Holy Spirit and dear people, brought the healing that I was seeking so desperately, just in the wrong way.

God's love truly does endure . . . forever. I don't always believe it or feel it, but it is true, nevertheless. Praise God for that!

You Are God

Verse
All that I am
All that I'll ever be
Is hidden in the mystery of You.

All that I have
All that I'll ever need
Everything I long to be is found in You.

Chorus
For You are God
And Your love endures forever
I lift my voice to sing Your praise.
I give my life to glorify Your name
'Cause there is nothing that I would rather do than worship You.

Bridge
When I've lost my way, Your love will guide me.
When darkness clouds my life, Your light will shine.
And when my heart is broken, Your comfort brings the healing that I need.

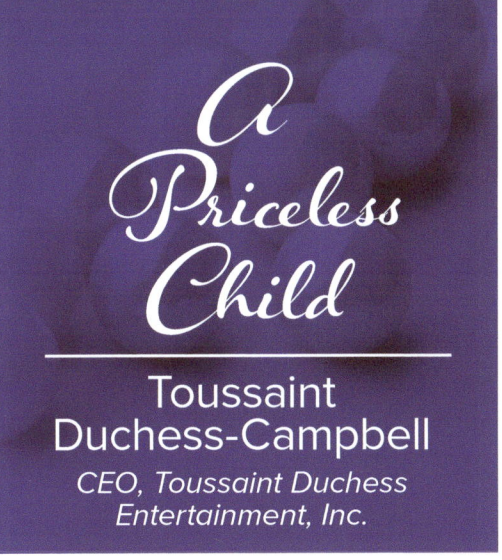

A Priceless Child

Toussaint Duchess-Campbell
CEO, Toussaint Duchess Entertainment, Inc.

As a young Christian woman pursuing a career as a Hollywood actress, I was desperately seeking fame and fortune, until one day I discovered I had to make a decision—the world or my soul. Unaware of my worth at the time, I was torn between glamour and wealth . . . and protecting my soul. In 1998, when I moved to Los Angeles, I had recently rededicated my life to God, but I didn't really understand my true worth. I was cute and I could act, so I convinced myself that my happiness was in the heart of Hollywood.

Only five months in the city, I landed one of Hollywood's most famous managers. I was at a Jamie Foxx show and a gentleman approached me, saying: "Hello, you are so pretty. You must be an actress"—the golden words every starving actress wishes to hear.

The following week I was in his Beverly Hills office signing a three-year contract! He seemed to believe in me. He paid for my photo shoots, acting classes, and commercial workshops. He also paid my rent and put extra cash in my pocket to help me take care of my son. I remember saying to my best friend, Jordan (R.I.P): "This is too good to be true!"

TRUE, it was. GOOD, it was not. The only audition offer I received from this alliance was: "Will you come to my house so we can discuss your career . . . tonight!" Turning down the offer twice, the third time I accepted. I gave Jordan the address and access code to the elaborate gated community, along with instructions to "Give me one hour and, if I'm not out, come and get me."

I was there only 35 minutes. His last words to me, before I left in tears: "In Hollywood, if you want something, you've got to give something." Storming out in disbelief, I headed back to my apartment crying so hard I could barely see the road. I called Jordan, who prayed and cried with me all the way home. In discovering my worth, I had to remind myself that I was a child of The Living God, covered by the blood of The Lamb . . . a Proverbs 31 woman whose price is far beyond that of rubies. I could not sell my soul to devil, because I belonged to the Kingdom, not Hollywood. I was, in fact, priceless.

I truly believe that experience, 15 years ago, was purposed just for me. I praise God for my inheritance in His Kingdom and for the strength I had to walk away from the devil's camp. When I did, my value increased. I felt like I had tried to sell a masterpiece painting on clearance, instead of the millions it was worth. That pivotal moment influences me to warn God's daughters not to give Hollywood, or anything else, the power to define their worth.

Today, I am blessed with a personal ministry that informs young people about the deceptive practices and destructive path too often inherent in the entertainment business. I also pride myself in strategically making a difference as I oversee the operations of my own new entertainment company whose motto is: "reaching the heart, mind and soul through entertainment."

Personal worth is intrinsic, measured solely by what we accept. The bottom line is to value yourself more, as we are all priceless. Your heart is a precious gift and your body is the temple of the Holy Spirit. It is not your own. Respect yourself, and demand that you be respected, in turn!

Know ye not that your body is the temple of the Holy Ghost which is in you, which ye have of God, and ye are not your own? For ye are bought with a price: therefore glorify God in your body, and in your spirit, which are God's.
— 1 Corinthians 6:19-20

The Words That Matter Most

Dana Evans
Educator

I recall my high school experience as one typical of most adolescents traversing through the throes of puberty. These prepubescent moments of intense change are a true microcosm of our later experiences—those that require us to change and evolve, and molding us into what we will become. This ebb and flow in the movement of life is a dance that replays in our lives again and again. And, our responses to the changes, not the challenges themselves, direct our victories . . . or our failures.

One day, I was summoned to my high school counselor's office. She began by talking about students living up to their potential, and moved on to tell me that my standardized test scores were high. When questioned about my plans after graduation, I promptly replied: "College!" She encouraged me to attend a workshop the following week.

The workshop focus was as surprising as it was disappointing, and the reason why I've chosen to share this twist of fate. The workshop was for "women bricklayers!" Although I saw myself as a college graduate, she saw me as a bricklayer—one of my first experiences of my worth being challenged. Yet, today I believe her words to be prophetic.

It's 2014, and my dream to become a college graduate is a reality. In fact, I now have a Ph.D. from a top-ranked university and managed to graduate with a 3.9 grade point average. But, the ebb and flow of life again has reared its head, and I am facing one of the most pervasively devastating challenges of my life. I am a principal. Or, I was a principal in Atlanta Public Schools. I am now part of an ongoing investigation of the "CRCT cheating scandal" as it's been referred to for the last five years. The CRCT is a battery of tests administered throughout Georgia that tests the knowledge of first through eighth graders in core subject areas.

In 2007, I was the principal of a middle school ranked as one of the highest performing schools in the state. An excerpt from my first letter to the staff reads:

> "The enormity of the challenges we face (as educators) resounds in our minds, and we sometimes feel powerless to the will of the harsh conditions of the world – things like poverty, lack of parental support, unmotivated students, etc. I've come to realize, however, we are not powerless. Exactly the opposite—Maya Angelou said we are "powerful beyond measure." I, wholeheartedly, believe that. In each of us is a predetermined purpose that has the ability to create the positive change we want to see in the world and in our school."

More than mere words, my message represented a cultivated belief that resonated with every decision I made as a leader. But, little did I know I would be writing another letter four years later to bid my staff a fond farewell.

Ironically, the time has come for me to live out the "bricklayer prophesy"—to become that bricklayer, but not one of mortar and clay. The bricks I lay are words to renew and replace the negative words we use with words that encourage and build, lead you to your purpose, draw you closer to God, and allow you to see the light of understanding your true worth.

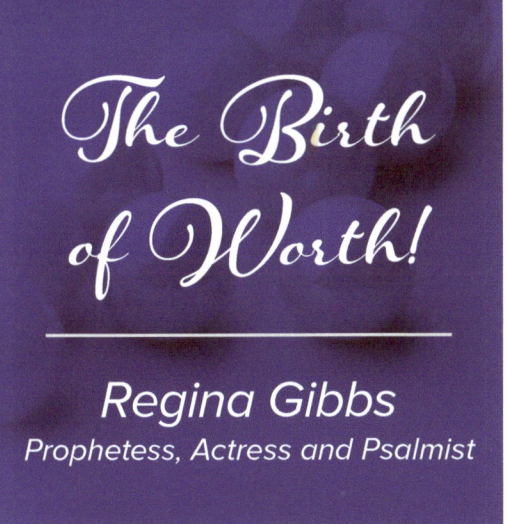

The Birth of Worth!

Regina Gibbs
Prophetess, Actress and Psalmist

My life journey has been one hell of a ride, from age 5 to, now, 50. Experiencing situations that became defining moments of discovery caused me to search deeply for my identity. At the age of five, a very tragic moment impacted my life. An accident, which left me in a coma for days, began the journey. By age seven, I had critical emergency surgery. By twelve, my life was darkened by severe depression after losing my mom to a massive heart attack. Not even a teenager yet, I was on an emotional roller coaster. These circumstances created issues in my life. I struggled with my identity. Not knowing who I was blocked truth—my personal truth—about my essence, which resulted in doubt, discouragement, dysfunction and distraction. These were the four "Ds" that set up a door of death for me. Wow, I said it!

At fourteen, I became sexually active and my life spiraled out of control: promiscuity, teenage pregnancy, manipulation and other self-inflicted wounds. I made choices from a lonely place of wanting to be validated and to belong. I had a deep void in my life and filled the void with what I thought was love. I equated love with compassion—compassion of lust from the first boy that showed it to me. Love can manifest itself in a variety of ways, but love, real love, doesn't entice you to compromise your worth.

Love elicits a variety of different feelings, states of being and attitudes that arise from interpersonal affection. It can refer to an emotion of strong attraction and personal attachment. It can also be a virtue, representing human kindness, compassion and affection—"the unselfish loyal and benevolent concern for the good of another." It may also describe compassionate and affectionate actions towards other humans, oneself or animals. The Greek definition for love is friendship (*philia*), sexual and/or romantic desire (*eros*), and self-emptying or divine love (*agape*). The love I needed was the love of my own worth—the love of God!

Knowing my worth would have saved me from experiencing low self-esteem and a mental breakdown. I ran out of options, but God proved His love by saving me. I surrendered to God and He showed me who He chose me to be. The anointing is expensive and the process can feel "crushing." Why? Because the anointing changes lives—it gives life!

Choosing to walk out my destiny disappointed many people who no longer benefited from my poor decision making. You can't be who you are and who you were at the same time! You must leave your past and run toward your future. Master your mind. Master your life. Shift your thinking. Change your mindset. And, enlarge your expectations. Create an opening for a greater vision. Then, open your vision to release the limitations that position your life for the manifestation of what was originally decreed by God. When you "become," you begin to fulfill purpose. Fulfilling purpose, creating destiny agreement, and agreeing with destiny accelerates the abundant life God has promised.

Question: How many times have you held on to what you should have let go, and let go of what you should have held on to? Your ability to choose wisely is in the strength of knowing your worth. And, your worth will stand before you, eternally, as a perpetual and glistening mirror that reflects your "power to win!"

Mantel. Message. Mandate. Movement. Method. Moment.
God will position the mantel, speak the message, call forth the mandate, empower the movement, strategize the method, and create the moment. Dare to be determined!

www.reginagibbs.org

Young Believer: Growing in My Worth

India Hunt
Rising Star

I'm only 13. I haven't been through major, life-changing events in my life yet. I'm still learning the ways and purpose of my existence. When I think about my worth at this point of my life, I think about why I was placed on earth. I wonder what has God has planned for me. I ask myself: What gifts has God given me to share and help others? How can I use these gifts to make the world a better place? What is there about me that is special and unique? How has God favored me?

Music? Maybe music is how I help others. I love music. I love to sing. I love to put people in a better mood, no matter what they might be going through. But, of course, music uses emotions. It craves emotions. Emotions expressed while singing come from things you have been through, your past. I'm still learning how to fit all the pieces together—how to pull everything I can from my small triumphs and put them into my performances. I'm still building on developing the type of connection I need to make between me and every audience I'm blessed to sing for. I want to make people feel moved by my singing—to make them feel like they are not alone. I want them to know that someone does care.

Friendship? Maybe my gift is being truthful with the advice I give to others. It may sound silly, but being the same age as my friends gives me an advantage. I understand what they are going through as they leave childhood behind to become teenagers. I'm there for them when they need me, and even when they don't know that they need me. I listen to them, and then I try to help to the best of my ability. Even if they don't like what I say at the time, later on they are grateful. I'd rather be a real friend and tell the truth than be a nice friend who won't be upfront with you. I believe if you're always told what you want to hear, you'll never learn anything.

Permission to grow? Maybe my gift to me is allowing myself to grow into the woman God is calling me to be. I am growing daily and strive to live by what the Bible says. A lot of things the Bible teaches are lessons that are hard to follow, like forgiveness, or being kind to those you are not particularly fond of. It is hard to forgive certain people; especially people you have trusted so dearly, yet, they stabbed you in the back. It is even more difficult to love your enemies and not let the contempt they hold inside corrupt you and cause you to resort to stooping down to their level.

They can be the most annoying, rude, unlikeable creatures on earth, but you never know what they may be going through that is causing them to be that way. They may be experiencing some pain, some problems at home, or bullying at school. You just never know the burdens other people bear; and as young people, just like me, they may not have the tools yet to deal with all the challenges life is putting in their paths. One thing I've realized is that everyone makes mistakes. No one is perfect.

I guess it all pays off in the long run. So, for me, my worth can be many things. Over time it will become clearer to me. All I can do is let God guide me.

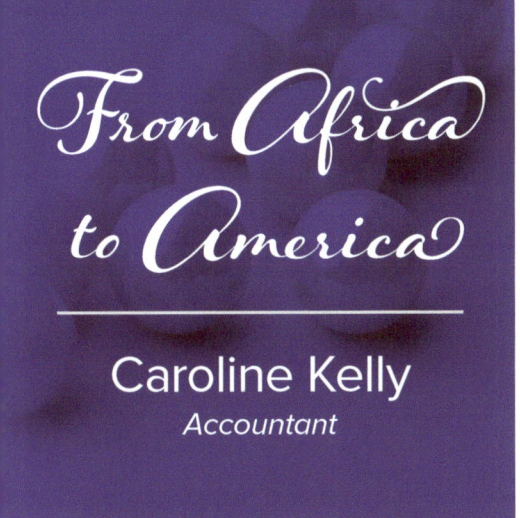

From Africa to America

Caroline Kelly
Accountant

In 1994, I journeyed from Nairobi, Kenya, to the United States as a survivor of domestic violence—thankful to God I was able to get away. Even though my divorce was messy and challenging, I refused to let that define me. The day I landed on American soil I cried out to God, asking Him to cover me. It was at that moment I felt as though a tremendous weight had been lifted off me, and I knew I had to press on.

You see, when you've been a victim of domestic violence at some point you begin to believe the lie the perpetrator has cast upon you—that you're worthless. But, somewhere deep inside my soul I always knew my life would be better than what it was. I knew God had more in store for me; I just needed to know the "how." Even though parts of my life were ripped and torn, I had two young beautiful daughters for whom I wanted to live.

The hand of God began to move in my life like never before. I am now remarried, have gained a daughter and a son through marriage, and my husband and I were blessed with a beautiful daughter who is now 8 years old. Today, I am a successful accountant with my own practice, and some of my clients are my fellow compatriots. God kept me grounded in my rich roots, while uprooting me to thrive on new ground. He does things like that!

When I started my part-time business in 1999, on my kitchen table, I worked countless hours building my clientele in a country that was new to me. I knew God gave me the gift of effectively managing numbers, but it was in my struggle that He equipped me with the gift of perseverance. I was confident I had what it took to survive, and I used everything in me to make it happen. By the end of 2001, my client base blossomed and I had to find an office location. Yes, the woman who took shelter in an unknown country emerged as a successful business woman with an office AND clients!

Leaving the corporate world and working for myself, full-time, was scary. But, I trusted God to expand my business. He did, and He continues to do so. My life is a still journey. I guess all our lives are. It hasn't been easy to get to the place where I am right now; there have been many challenges and stumbling blocks. But, I chose not to get discouraged, as I diligently sought the lessons in these pearls of wisdom:

- Strive to be better than you were the day before.
- Be honest with yourself and with others.
- Take on life with passion.
- Keep dreaming and dream big with eyes wide open.
- God only expects you to have faith to take the first step, even if you don't see the rest of the staircase.
- God will make your dreams come true.
- Have faith the size of a mustard seed and watch God work.
- No matter where you're from, your dreams are valid.

Knowing and loving God has been the most rewarding gift ever. I know when I leave my problems and concerns in His magnificent hands He will work to fix them for me. The enemy toiled with me in the form of endless worry, day in and day out. But, I finally got it. Actually, God's got it!

My Alabaster Box

Gwendolyn Knight
Registered Nurse

"Everything will be okay," are the words I hear as my truck loses control, seeming to tumble in slow motion with my belongings in turmoil, as if I am in the path of a tornado. Boom! After rolling over several times, my truck stops. I hear my friends' deafening cries, screaming for help and calling for Jesus. It's dark. I'm awake. I'm alive. But, wait! I can feel my injuries and all I can do is pray: "Please God, don't let me die like this!" This is not a story about me, or a story of tragedy, but a message about a second chance to be an example, a catalyst for change, and a chance to be a light and give God all honor and praise.

Singing has been a passion my entire life. I sang my first solo at the age of six and continued in concert and church choirs during grade school. After high school, I attended Bethune-Cookman University where I was introduced to their concert chorale—a world-renowned organization.

While participating in the choir, I was invited to become part of a ministry called Victors for Christ. This group of sophomores sang for various functions at school and local churches. On October 19, 2007, during my senior year, Victors for Christ was invited to sing at an out-of-town church. I was driving, along with four band members, and we were extremely late due to weather and traffic conditions. I got out of the truck to see how far the traffic stretched, hopped back in and resumed driving, forgetting to refasten my seatbelt. Within moments I lost control of the vehicle—it jerked to the left, then to the right, veering off onto the grassy shoulder and, finally, flipping over several times.

Ejected and pinned underneath the truck, I moved in and out of consciousness. I finally woke up to fire and rescue responders calling my name and pulling me from the wreckage. On the way to the hospital, although I could barely breathe, I recall singing Lamar Campbell's "Total Adoration." My injuries included three hip fractures, broken teeth, a broken right arm, internal bleeding, multiple abrasions and a crushed left leg. Yet, I was so grateful to be alive. Eventually, gangrene consumed my leg, leaving me as an above-the-knee, left leg amputee. On a ventilator, tubes inserted into both nostrils, a wound vac connected to my residual limb, and hundreds of staples holding my flesh in place, I was discolored, disheartened and disgusted. Here I was, 22 years old in my senior year of nursing school, marriage on the rocks and now an amputee. I felt ugly—as if I were going to die.

My faith waivered. Women tried to weasel their way into the arms of my husband, underestimating my abilities as a wife due to my new disability. Then, God brought me back to Romans 8:28: " . . . all things work together for good for those who love God." Released from the hospital the day before Thanksgiving, I returned to school in January using a wheelchair. I graduated from college with a Bachelor of Science degree in nursing exactly six months after this ordeal, and walked across the stage to accept my degree to a standing ovation.

The storms raging in your life aren't only stepping stones for you, they are also tools to uplift others. Today, I am a senior staff registered nurse at two of the leading hospitals in the nation, a wife and a mother of two incredible children. But, most important, I am a servant of the Lord. Through God's miracle, I am able to minister to patients and coworkers. This is a story of second chances. God, I pour my written praises to you like oil. All glory and honor belong to you.

The Joys of Motherhood

Deidré Pratt & Cameron Sample

Be there . . .
Hug them.
Know where they are physically and emotionally.
Be their number one fan.
Pray with them.
Guide them.
Teach them.
Respect them.
Support them.
Speak blessings over them.
Laugh with them. Laugh with them, often.
Protect them.
Love them unconditionally.
Correct them.
Embrace them.
Celebrate their uniqueness.
Dream with them.
Nurture their vision, goals, and aspirations.
Believe in them.
Honor them.
Be there . . . .

Let the Circle Be Unbroken

As I read this impassioned collection of essays by women of all ages, from all walks of life—sometimes with tears in my eyes, other times with bursts of joy's laughter—at every moment I experienced ineffable feelings and a tremendous sense of pride in the resilience and greatness of womanhood. The intimate and sacred moments of these indomitable women are unmasked as they tell their stories, share their hearts, acknowledge their missteps and rejoice in their victories—not for their glory, but so that your life, my life, can be impacted and stirred to recognize our worth within.

...in Pursuit of Women's Worth

These are the gallant women who journeyed deep into those places they never imagined they would revisit, places where their memories were buried, healed and dusted off, or prayed to be forgotten—not for their glory, but so that your life, my life, would be penetrated by their souls and experiences in ways that would reshape, deliver, and inspire. These are the incredible women who resolved to share their fear turned faith, sickness turned health, tragedies turned triumphs, good turned great, and better turned best—the selfless circle of women who contributed to this momentous and timeless body of literary authenticity in celebration of women's worth.

Deidré Pratt
Founder and President
My Worth Ministries, Inc.

Tender Seedlings of Worth

Choices
Zaria Davis

It's important for me to make good small choices today because it will help me make good big decisions when I grow up. Some of the good choices I make today are paying attention in class, completing my homework, being kind to my little brother and my sisters, and doing what my mom tells me to do. She loves us so much and shows us every day. This means a lot to me and it makes me more confident. At night time, before I go to bed, I take time to pray and ask God to guide me in all that I do. I set an example with my friends because I know that I am a leader. I am off to a great start to being all that God wants me to be. Yes, I am worth it!

Train up a child in the way he should go, and when he is old he shall not depart from it.

– Proverbs 22:6

Purpose
Ava Prince

My mommy prayed for God to bless her with a beautiful child. God answered her prayer! I know that I am here for a special reason. I am only 6 years old, but I know that I will do something really great one day. I am a bundle of joy, and everyone smiles when I am around. I am a gift. Yes, I am worth it!

For I know the thoughts that I think toward you, says the Lord, thoughts of peace and not of evil, to give you a future and a hope.

– Jeremiah 29:11

All-Star
Tia Williams

I can do it all! I go to school every day and I focus on what my teachers tell me to do. I make great grades. I take swim lessons and that is so much fun! I also played basketball and soccer last year on co-ed boys and girls little teams. That was a lot of work and it was hot. My mom loves to cook and bake for friends and clients, and when she is in the kitchen I get to help her out. This makes me happy. My mom and dad truly love me, and they are so glad that I am strong and healthy. See, when I was born, I was so tiny (2 lbs. 4 oz.) that my dad's wedding band fit loosely around my arm. Look at me now—pretty, smart and doing it all. Yes, I am worth it!

I can do all things through Christ who strengthens me.

– Philippians 4:13

There is No Rainbow Without a Little Rain

Grace Lee
University Admissions Counselor

People are like stained-glass windows. They sparkle and shine when the sun is out, but when the darkness sets in their true beauty is revealed only if there is a light from within.

– Elisabeth Kubler-Ross

One of my personal struggles is dealing with depression, sometimes getting overwhelmed with high expectations from family or putting pressure on myself. In the past, there have been times when these negative thoughts became too much to bear and I have wanted to kill myself.

As an outgoing and popular person who loves being around people, I was crowned homecoming queen during my senior year of college. However, I still have dark moments of feeling very lonely—rough patches of "ups and downs." But, what helps me more than anything is focusing on God's love for me. Realizing how many blessings I have, instead of focusing on my inadequacies, has helped me tremendously in dealing with my daily struggles of being too hard on myself.

This is an issue for many people who don't want to address it, don't believe it's important, or don't know how to successfully deal with it. But, you can't allow these negative thoughts to consume your life. You have to know and believe in your heart that you are worthy, that you are loved.

I am a work in progress, but through God's grace alone He has brought me so far. The strength and confidence I now have in celebrating my own worth is all because of Him. Through my struggles and weaknesses, I find strength in God who gives me peace, understanding and love. I am learning to understand the light I have from within. God is revealing so many things to me right now in my life, making me vulnerable to my inability to be strong on my own.

So, don't fight your fight of depression, drug addiction, alcoholism, or whatever struggles you are facing alone, because you are not alone. God is there with you, every step of the way. Pray for peace. Pray to find your self-worth. And, pray to let go of things that are not benefiting you. Let go of your distractions and the things that are hurting you. Instead, just focus on God and the love He has for you. Start from there.

God is most glorified in us when we are most satisfied in Him.

– John Piper

Self-worth is understanding the gifts and talents God has given you and using them to bless others. Shine from within, and know just how wonderful and beautiful you are. Beautiful . . . not defined by your outward appearance, but by the measure of your heart to love others, to accept others just as they are, just how Christ loves us. But, you have to learn to love yourself before you can love others.

There is a reason for every single season. When you think everything is lost and you have no hope, just trust and have faith in God, knowing He has a plan. Don't look at challenges as times of despair, look at them as opportunities and blessings—that God is preparing you for something. There is no rainbow without a little rain. Life is 10% circumstances, 90% attitude. Life is 10% what happens to you, and 90% how you react to it!

Marana tha: Come, O Lord

Yoon Pender
Massage Therapist

God loves me. He shows me daily through a whisper or in deed His immeasurable love for me. He shows me daily my worth, simply because I am His daughter. My heart is entangled in His, and my life exemplifies one that seeks to know God more and more each day. Prayer is the key for me. Prayer—my daily posture—it is deliberate and it is constant. It is how I focus on my growing relationship with my Heavenly Father.

What do I pray about? Everything. Never underestimate the power of prayer! When the weight of the world is too much for me, I seek Him. It is a safe place. It is a place where I know my petitions are heard. It is a place where I surrender and release my cares unto God because He wants me to and He asks me to.

There have been so many times I have failed when I made my own plans and decisions, because I did not rely on God fully—only partially. In times like these, I pray for restoration and trust: "Lord strengthen my faith." I am simply asking God to show me how to trust Him for those things and situations for which I long. I am asking God to teach me how to trust His plan and His method for working out the details of my life. My favorite scripture that offers me comfort and the motivation to "let go and let God" is:

Trust in the Lord with all thine heart;
and lean not unto thine own understanding.
In all thy ways acknowledge Him, and
He shall direct thy paths.
– Proverbs 3:5-6

I believe no matter what the situation is in which I find myself, God will take care of me. I am His and he tells me that I am worth the best—His plan for my life. Why? Because he loves me! Another favorite scripture that assures me of His love and declares my worth to Him is:

For I am persuaded that neither death, nor life, nor angels,
nor principalities, nor power, nor things present, nor things to come,
nor height, nor depth, nor other creatures shall be able to separate us
from the Love of God, which is in Christ Jesus our Lord.
– Romans 8:38-39

Yes! The depth of God's love for me and you is immeasurable beyond our own understanding—beyond imagination and experiences—in so much that He died for us so that we may live with Him forever and ever and ever. Amen.

For God sent not His Son into the world to condemn
the world, but that the world through Him might be saved.
– John 3:17

To me, this is the good news! Lord, come quickly. *Marana tha . . . .*

In the Garden
Deidré Pratt
Founder and President, My Worth Ministries, Inc.

Yes, it's true. Sometimes, life strikes us with us unfair blows. Too often we've seen, heard and been subjected to too much . . . for too long. Family, friends, and society can plant seeds of destruction in our lives without even realizing it. As we grow from little children to adults, those destructive seeds can flourish within us. And, our core becomes entangled in the vines of those seeds planted long ago.

Our lives evolve, yet we are unable to fully enjoy the blessings God has given us. We have no deep-rooted joy and contentment. Our very foundation is tainted—tainted with the poison of a little girl or boy who's been exposed to all the wrong things. We attempt to figure out the source of our pain, and the inner battle begins. Life-changing answers to must-asked questions are sought: Who will stay in my core? Who must I ask to leave? And, whom must I leave? What will remain with me? Honest answers to these questions are critical as we work to reestablish our personal truths.

The process begins.

There is much work to be done to recreate our new garden of life. There will be times we will want to stop and give in. We can't. Giving in or giving up is not an option. Cultivation is about our purpose, our destiny, and everyone and every great plan tied to it. We must pray for strength to remain committed. When we get tired, let's rest if we must; but let's rest in God's hands. It takes a lot of guts to confront the inner self. It takes a winning mindset to even consider the task! Let's embrace the good that is already coming forth.

Blooming.

Hey! See the light? Continue to follow the light. It's God's compass in the midnight hour. Do you hear the voice? Yes, that still voice. That's God's voice leading us, even when the clouds are gray and dreary. And oh, those other voices, the ones that sound so familiar, so loud? Those are voices of praise. Praise from all of those connected to our deliverance—our covenant connectors! So, you've never heard of a covenant connector? Covenant connectors are all of those who saw the greatness in you and believed in you when you couldn't even trust yourself. Now, there is one more sound. I hear it, do you? Yes, that one! That is your praise! You are gleaming because heaven's victory celebration is in honor of you.

Take a look at us! Look at the majesty of our garden! Look at the offshoots of all we took the time to plant and protect. Now, we should really stop for a moment. Let's smell and savor the aroma of our garden and command that God is good! Finally, we are refusing to live our lives through the mind and heart of a wounded child.

I know there were times when we thought we were all alone. Yet, while we thought we were alone, others were on their journey to victory the same time we were. They arrived right before us and, because they were not afraid to share their struggles and their victories, we are able to see, firsthand, if they could survive, we can too!

A word of caution . . .

We can't get so caught up in the newness that we forget from where God has brought us. We must look back, and share, and be real, because someone else is right behind us, and barely holding on.

Your Covenant Connector,
Deidré

God's Promise

Alexis Prince
Business Analyst

My heart's desire was to one day become a mother and embrace the hugs and kisses of a sweet, beautiful baby. To have a child was not only my desire, it was also a sacred promise from the Lord—God's promise to me that gave me hope and tested my faith.

During my first marriage, I became pregnant several times. Each time it was short lived. There was miscarriage after miscarriage. I felt as if I were on an emotional roller coaster, begging the conductor to stop the ride so I could wake up from what seemed to be a nightmare. "Why? Why? Why am I not able to carry a child?" Then it happened. I heard God's still, but clear, voice in my spirit: "I will not give you a child with him, but when I do, it will be great." God had made a promise to me! He was going to give me a child, but it was not going to be with my current husband, and I understood the reason.

You see, my first marriage was not full of the happy marital bliss most young girls dream about when they fantasize about their "knight in shining armor." It was far from that. While there were some good times together, our marriage was darkened by the uncontrollable rage my husband battled from within. Too often, I was the outlet for his emotionally and physically abusive rage. But, God had a better plan for my life, and divorce followed.

Two years later, I met my now, wonderful, husband of ten years. A few years after we married, we were pregnant! Weeks went by and I did not miscarry. Was this the fulfillment of God's promise? But then it happened . . . we miscarried at four months. After a period of dealing with the devastation, I made the decision to continue to believe God's promise, to stand on His word, in spite of it all.

Putting faith into action, I started preparing the nursery room. I bought clothes, furniture and various baby items. Something in me just knew we would have a girl. I even chose her name—Ava. Over her bed, I hung a plaque with the letters A-V-A.

One Sunday, my husband, James, visited a church in our area while I was out of town. During the service, he went up for prayer. The pastor told my husband that God said "No more miscarriages." The pastor asked about me and James told him I was out of town. He said, "Tell her that God said no more miscarriages."

When I came home, I was overwhelmed by what I heard. James and I put our faith into action (wink). Weeks went by and it was time for my annual routine doctor's visit. After my examination, my doctor, who knew my story, came back into the room beaming: "Alexis, you're pregnant!" he said. This time, I knew things were different and I was elated. I asked him how far along I was and he calculated the conception date back to the night God said: "No more!"

On April 2, 2009, Ava Prince was born, weighing 4 lbs. 15 oz.! She was healthy. She was strong. My Ava, God's promise, was here!

My worth is cradled in God's hands, and I am, eternally, in His favor. It looked like I was barren. It looked like I could not carry a child. However, I chose to believe otherwise.

What promise has God whispered in your ear? No matter the circumstances, believe God's promise over your life. Walk daily in faith and believe Him at His word.

A Journey of Trust

Adia Randall
College Student

The summer of 2013 was the summer before my senior year of high school. As a student-athlete, my heart was set on attending a large academic and athletic powerhouse in the South. My list soon narrowed to the universities of Georgia, Florida, Alabama, and Auburn University. That June, I visited and fell in love with Auburn; every little thing seemed amazing to me. From the moment I stepped foot on the campus, I knew this was where I wanted to spend the next four years of my life . . . and I simply claimed it! There was no reason to look any further.

During my visit to Auburn, I immediately began completing their application for Early Admission—the longest and most stressful thing I ever had to do. Realizing that the fate of my future was on the line, I also realized that I needed help. With guidance from the Lord and my mom, I finished the application and began the long and tortuous waiting game.

I continued to tell everyone that Auburn was my destiny because I knew that God had never failed me. Whenever I found myself thinking about Auburn I would pray. He had blessed those around me with so many miracles, I knew He could get me into Auburn if I only believed and had faith that this was where the Lord wanted me to go.

Months went by and my letter of acceptance still had not arrived. My mom, forever "the voice of reason," encouraged me to consider some other schools, so I reluctantly took a tour of Georgia Southern. Nice school. Nice visit. But, it wasn't Auburn. Anxiously texting my mom from the Georgia Southern campus, I told her: "No school will ever compare to Auburn!" Her simple reply offered me both encouragement and comfort: "The Lord will give you the desires of your heart." That was all I needed to get my head back on track and remember my worth to God.

Before we left for church the following Sunday, my stepfather shared that he was being called to preach Sunday's word just for me . . . a word about trusting in the Lord. When the sermon ended and I went up for prayer, he quietly and caringly whispered in my ear: "Everything is going to work out just fine."

The following week was just as stressful—three Advanced Placement tests, a retake of the ACT college entrance exam, after-school practices for a chorus concert, and several make-up quizzes. On my way to one of the quizzes I got two weird calls: my stepdad instructing me to get home ASAP, and my aunt offering me "Congratulations!" I didn't have time to talk, or even think about what they were talking about. My focus was on the make-up quiz that my final grade depended on and the first semester of my senior year being over!

I arrived home to the biggest and best surprise of my life. After four months of waiting, I finally had received my acceptance letter to Auburn on the last day, of the last week, of my first semester of senior year. I was now holding in the palm of my hand the next chapter of my life. God did it again! He proved my worth to Him by giving me the desires of my heart and setting me on a righteous path to prepare and give back in His almighty name.

Trust in the Lord with all your heart and lean not on your own understanding; in all your ways submit to Him, and He will make your paths straight.

— Proverbs 3:5-6

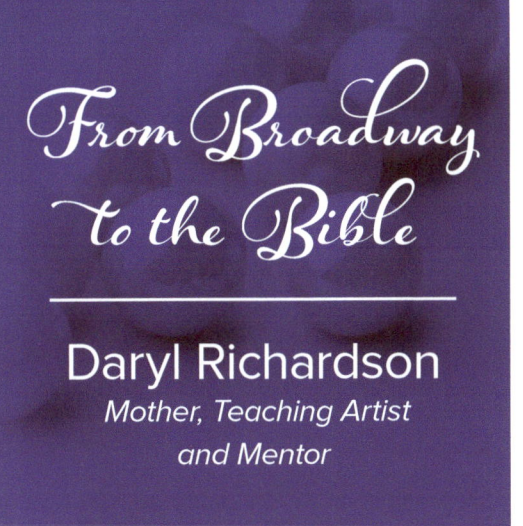

From Broadway to the Bible

Daryl Richardson
Mother, Teaching Artist and Mentor

Allow me to introduce myself. I am a native New Yorker and professional dancer of stage, film and television. I am also a director, producer, self-published author and caterer as well as the founder and CEO of The Me Nobody Knows—a nonprofit community-based organization based in Queens, New York, that has conducted programs in more than 17 schools throughout New York City.

Affectionately known as "Ms. Daryl," I am committed to bringing my expertise back to my community through the work of my organization. Targeting youth, by way of the arts, education, mentorship and empowerment, we dedicate ourselves to conducting programs that utilize the entire physical, singing, dancing, walking and talking self of every child in order for a well-balanced child to emerge.

Let me share with you two of the poems from my book, *Poems By The Spirit*—a volume of poetry that depict life's challenges, choices and oppositions, while offering solutions through prayer, wisdom, love, honor and forgiveness.

The Best Man

I know a man who's 35
But at times I think he's 10
He's a man of God who loves the Lord
And he says that he's born again

But the Bible says a tree is judged
By all of its good fruit
Is he hiding behind his Mercedes Benz
His good looks and his suit

But all these things shall pass away
And God shall judge his heart
Is he being all that God is calling him to
Or is he afraid to yield and do his part

Am I desiring this man
Is he God's choice for my life
You see, God knows I've been praying
To become someone's wife.

God Ordained, or Flesh and Blood

A man shall leave his parents
And to his wife he'll cleave
What God has joined together
Is apparent you're not to leave.

But there is a discrepancy
Let's talk about divorce
Did God ordain the marriage
Or was it flesh and blood enforced?

Copyright © 2010
Poems By The Spirit

Inside my heart beats the soul of a performer. In addition to numerous Broadway and film appearances, I have toured with well-known artists such as Babyface, Barry White, and Earth, Wind and Fire and been featured in numerous commercials and videos. As a choreographer, my work has included *Deliver the Dance, Children of God Tell Hell I Ain't Coming*, and Bishop TD Jakes' stage play, *Woman Thou Art Loosed*, directed by Tyler Perry. I also assisted the late Tony Award winner Gregg Burge in choreographing Michael Jackson's video, *Bad*.

I give glory to God for my abundant talents, gifts and opportunities, realizing that my ministry is wherever I tread my feet . . . inside and outside the four walls of the church. Prior to this place of revelatory knowledge, I experienced many trials and tribulations. It was the very process of life that made me realize what it truly means to serve God. When you lay down your life, God will resurrect all of who you are for His ordained purpose and destiny.

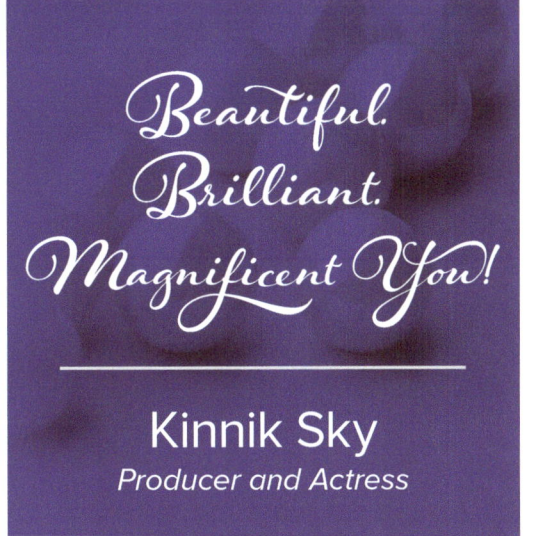

Beautiful. Brilliant. Magnificent You!

Kinnik Sky
Producer and Actress

My journey has been one of preparation, hard work, opportunity and the Lord's blessing. As a veteran of stage, film and television, I have performed in more than 30 stage plays over the last 15 years. Award-winning directors and producers Tyler Perry, Robert Townsend, and Kenny Leon have each cast me in their respective projects, tapping into both my vocal range and acting ability. My major theatre credits include *Dreamgirls*, *For Colored Girls* and *Madea's Class Reunion*, and I was a Top 13 finalist on the mega-hit show, *American Idol*.

My experience in the business led me to launch my own production company, Dazzal Mi Entertainment. Yet, my proudest accomplishment to date is writing, producing and starring in the stage production *Sunday Mourning*, which won seven NAACP Theater Award nominations and three NAACP Theater Awards. Above all, God has been good to me by empowering me to recognize my own value, my own worth.

Knowing your worth is one of the most powerful tools in the human experience. It's like perspective. It can change your life in an instant. For some, it takes a plethora of experiences. For others, the validation necessary to feel empowered and valuable has always existed. More often than not, the latter is a result of great parental guidance. It's not to say that those of us who need life experiences to truly understand the diamond that we are did not have great parental guidance. It just means that each of us is made differently.

Differences are what makes this world amazing. Can you imagine how boring life would be if we were all the same? Thank God, we are not! Thank God, we are all a unique design created by a Master who never runs out of ideas. Each idea is as brilliant as the next. How wonderful is the moment that we truly understand our unique brilliance in the design called "YOU." Called me. Called the amazing. Called the gifted. Called the wonderful. Called the beautiful . . . the magnificent.

Whether you're a writer, teacher, homemaker, or doctor . . . a high school dropout, college graduate, teen mother, single woman, scholar, minister, or even a prophet, there is a brilliance that exists only in you. There is something so unique, so grand and so special that only you can offer it to the world. What if I told you that it only can be found if you stop judging yourself, comparing yourself, doubting yourself and wondering if you are truly worthy to shine? How can you not be worthy to shine when you were created in the image of the most high? THE. MOST. HIGH.

There is none higher than the one who created you—your likeness. When you are ready to step into the calling that is you, your life, your soul, this world will be better because of it. Understand your worth. Embrace your worth. Do not settle for anything less than your worth. Scream it from a mountain top, or whisper it in the darkness of night. It's all the same. Own it. Beautiful. Brilliant. Magnificent. YOU.

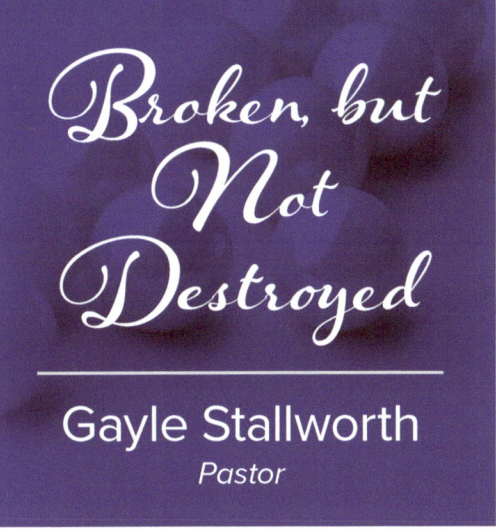

Broken, but Not Destroyed

Gayle Stallworth
Pastor

Born the ninth child of thirteen siblings to the late Bishop Lewis D. Stallworth, Sr. and Mary M. Stallworth, I was very shy and quiet as a child. I avoided conflict and confusion as much as possible. Yet, at an early age, I learned that no matter how much I intended to be well behaved, it did not control the behavior of others.

At the age of 19, I married and planned to stay married. But, after four children and fourteen years, it ended in a horrible divorce that made me feel tattered and broken. Bitterness, hatred and self-doubt took over and became an ever-present factor in my life. The shame of divorce, the suffering of my children, and the decline in my walk with Christ created a burden so heavy it seemed to be irreversible and impossible to overcome.

During this period of darkness and despair, I happened to hear a church elder preach, "Who shall separate us from the love of God?" This marked the beginning of my chains falling off. When I made up my mind to trust God and move forward my life has never been the same.

Believe it or not, my greatest pain transformed into what became my greatest victory. Every tear I have shed has now become a reservoir of praise and honor to my God. Each negative experience has endowed me with a double portion of anointing and the courage to help snatch someone else out of the bottomless pit of hell. The sufferings I endured have, ironically, become the source of my strength.

Despite hearing elders always say, "It's working for your good," I didn't see it while I was going through it. But, I've found it to be absolutely true. I have been given the ministry of "helps," including ministering restoration to the weak, healing for the wounded, and sharing the peace of God with broken hearts and troubled souls. I know it might not look like it right now, but you shall recover all, and you can survive anything with the help of God. I did, and my future looks brighter than ever!

After I went through the storms of life, I was still blessed to earn a Bachelor of Science degree in business management from the University of Phoenix and a Bachelor of Arts degree from the Ministerial Training Institute in Inglewood, California. Currently, I am enrolled in the Master of Education in Educational Leadership program at Concordia University in Portland, Oregon. And, most recently, I was elected the first female chairperson of the Pentecostal Churches of the Apostolic Faith International, where I am affectionately known as "Madam Chairlady."

It's simply amazing what God can do with broken pieces! Today, I travel throughout the country, speaking, teaching and preaching the Gospel to a lost and dying world. Once, I allowed my past to haunt me—to hold me back from reaching my fullest potential and discovering my worth—but now that I've been set free by the power of God there's no turning back.

God is good . . . all the time! He paved the way for me to reinvent myself—to embrace life and living with greater purpose and a renewed sense of vigor and vitality. He has given me the power, strength and vision to press toward the mark of the high calling of God in Christ Jesus. My greatest joy is to faithfully serve God's people; and I remain ready, willing and available for His service.

From an Army Soldier to God's Soldier

Sonja Stribling
Certified Life Coach

Born to Ruby, a housekeeper with a 3rd grade education, and Oscar Davis, a sharecropper, I was the youngest of 12 children. After having what she thought was her last child, at 45 my mother gave birth to me. By the time I came along, I think she was tired, so I pretty much had free rein to do whatever I wanted. At a young age, I was molested by a family member and touched inappropriately by another. At 15, I became pregnant and gave birth to a baby boy. At 16, I was raped and left for dead in a field.

As a young mother, I realized I had to leave the small town of Wilson, Arkansas, and better myself for my son. Thought to be "least likely to succeed," I earned a basketball scholarship. Immediately after college, I joined the U.S. Army. Within six months of enlisting, I was married and pregnant with my second son. Five years later, I gave birth to my third son. Married life was challenging for many reasons, but I didn't believe in divorce. My husband had been abused by his father and witnessed the abuse of his mother, physically and verbally, which left him with deep wounds and the curse continued.

My military career was on the rise. Moving up the ranks quickly, I attended Officer Candidate School. In 2006, I was deployed to Iraq. Immediately following a watch night service on January 1, 2007, I went to my room and laid my head on my pillow. Filled with love and peace, I had great expectations for the new year. Moments later, sirens sounded. I grabbed my M16 rifle and ran out to the bunker. The earth shook and the whistling sounds of gunfire and bombs rang out. This was the second time I could have lost my life, but God!

Fifteen months later, I came home from the war zone. Things seemed normal, but five months later I noticed a change. One day I felt faint and bizarre, as if my spirit had stepped out of my body and was standing over me saying "shake it off." Emotionally confused, I began experiencing severe anxiety attacks, which occurred almost daily and left me feeling like I was dying slowly inside. I finally shared with my husband the dark place in which I felt trapped. I needed his unyielding support, but he failed to step up. My body was physically and emotionally in turmoil and I was haunted by suicidal thoughts. It seemed unbearable, but prayer became my weapon. I recall spending hours on my knees talking to God, my whole body trembling with fear. "Lord, please don't leave me here to die," and God saw fit to save me once again.

After 18 years of mental abuse by a husband who was supposed to cover, love and care for me, he left me and our children to fend for ourselves. I stopped eating and dropped from size 4 to 0. I lost interest in everything, including life. The only thing that kept me alive was knowing my children depended on me to survive. It took two years before I finally "let go and let God."

During this period, I grew as a mother and a woman of God. I was given the gift of speaking in tongues, learning quickly how powerful this was to the outcome of my life. Not only did I survive the attacks of the enemy, I also became aware of my potential and my purpose. Today, I am a certified life coach and and soon will earn a doctorate in Christian counseling—the beginning of a life dedicated to help women understand God's purpose for them.

Blessed, after being broken . . . .

Walking by Faith

Stacey Uche
*Founder and CEO,
Sickle Cell Matters, Inc.*

At the tender age of nine, I received my first lesson of God's unyielding love. I learned that God actually listens to a child's prayer. Tired of going to the hospital for treatment of warts that regularly grew to cover my entire foot, one night I prayed an earnest prayer: "Lord, you said ask and you shall be given, so I'm asking you to heal me and remove these warts. Amen." The next morning I immediately looked at my foot to see if God heard my cry and discovered that every single wart was miraculously gone! No longer did I have to regularly visit the hospital to have my warts frozen. I learned very early in life that God so loved me He cared enough to answer my cry. It was then I knew how special I was in the eyes of the Lord and that with faith healing is possible.

As a child, my mother shared with me that I had sickle cell trait. She cautioned me against having children with a person who also has the trait because it could lead to my children having sickle cell disease. So, prior to my engagement at age 26, I asked my fiancé if he carried the trait. He quickly answered "No," but the soft whisper of the Holy Spirit said, "This is not so." Since past experiences taught me that the Holy Spirit is a great comforter who leads and guides us into all truth, I didn't totally accept my fiancé's answer. So, I questioned his mother, but in a different way: "Has Peter ever been tested for sickle cell? Does he have sickle cell trait?" She, too, answered with the same "No." Again, the Holy Spirit whispered, "It is not so." Although neither of them consciously knew that sickle cell trait ran through Peter's bloodline, God knew. Instead of listening to the voice of Holy Spirit, I accepted their answers as truth.

On August 21, 2001, my beautiful daughter Chelsea was born with sickle cell disease. While she was in my womb, I heard that soft, still voice say, "This is your gift." I asked God, "What is wrong with my baby?" No sooner than I asked, I felt peace and surrendered to trusting His words. Notwithstanding, the challenges of parenting a chronically ill child can be overwhelming. The depth and breadth of the pain she endures, and I endure in watching her, could overtake me were it not for my faith and submission.

One day, as I watched my child suffer through a painful episode in the hospital, I cried out to God: "Lord, why don't you heal her as you did for me? I know that you can." God's answer: "It is Chelsea's faith that will heal her, not yours." He taught me the true meaning of "And the peace of God, which passeth all understanding, shall keep your hearts and your minds in Christ Jesus" (Philippians 4:7). Despite the fact that I want Chelsea's healing today, I must trust in God as I did as a child.

The greatest lesson I have learned is that in the midst of insurmountable circumstances, God will give you the power to endure and a message to sustain you while you wait. I believe, like me, Chelsea will come to experience God's faithfulness and healing power at His appointed time.

God continues to walk and talk with me and tell me I am His own. Even when I fail to take heed to His voice, He remains faithful. He taught me at an early age that faith is the key that unlocks the door of healing and blessings. He reminded me as an adult to trust Him completely no matter what others say. These lessons have sealed my belief that I am valuable to God . . . and that my worth is priceless.

Strength, Worth and Joy are in His Dwelling Place

Diana Wagner
Director of Joy and Perspective for My Family

I've learned that discovering your deepest fear or greatest loss will help you understand how God's anointing can help you find joy and know your worth. My parents divorced when I was four years old, and my father left my life for more than a decade. The disruption of my family left me searching for joy, stability and security. Our family wasn't without love, nor the trinity. God, the Holy Spirit, and Jesus Christ were always in "it," and for this I am thankful.

However, I didn't abide in Jesus during young adulthood because I was busy and angry over the loss of my family. Sadness transformed into ambition fueled by anger. By age 25, I had an education, a successful career and a happy marriage. In my late 30s, a sermon made clear to me that I did not have a Christ-centered life. I was a believer and a requestor of miracles. My prayers were often a list of things I wanted Him to do for me. I was a very worldly, an employee, a wife and mother of two, but I was also an immature Christian. I needed change!

I committed to joining a Bible study. By the time I completed the study, I concluded that God was calling me to leave my career and focus on Him and my family. I heard Him clearly saying that I would not be able to deal with unresolved issues in my character, nor would I ever achieve the plan He had for me unless I committed to trusting God and following His calling to leave my career and walk with Him.

The years immediately following God's calling were key to my growth and understanding of my worth and attainment of joy. Through reading God's word, I gained a clear sense of who I am in Christ and about God's promises. I discovered that I was overly attached to my goals and I didn't trust others. I had the "American Dream," but I was so weary and lacked the energy to enjoy my "great" life.

The study of God's word showed me that fear had been a motivating factor for me. I have recently replaced that fear with love and trust in God. It is important to note that leaving a job or career isn't something I recommend for everyone seeking to find something they have lost. Only God really knows how to show us to unearth the treasures He has buried in our souls.

For me, leaving my career was key to my discovering three worldly lies. The first lie was that my education, career and financial well-being would provide me with stability, security and joy. Secondly, that my worth was tied to my salary and the things that I could accomplish. Thirdly, that not needing anyone or counting on anyone was a virtue. However, the moment I made a focused decision to accept Christ as my Heavenly Father, things began to change in my life. My father returned after more than a decade of absence, explaining himself and tearfully asking for my forgiveness, which I gave freely and openly.

I have shared this beautiful and personal story of forgiveness with my children, and how important, possible and glorious it is to forgive others as Christ forgives us. My obedience has paid off financially and emotionally. Best of all, my joy and worth are tied to my new career as God's woman. It pays in ways of value and meaning: sweet "out loud" prayers that float from the lips of my children at meal and bed times, the many ways my husband demonstrates how much he appreciates me, the laughter that hangs like a melody around our home, the gift of being able to worship Him with every part of our lives, and the ability to lead others to Christ—to share His love and blessings with others.

Breaking the Silence of Child Sexual Abuse

Angela Williams
Founder and CEO, Voice Today, Inc.

Mommy, it hurts.
What hurts?
He hurts. He hurts me, Mommy.
How does he hurt you?
He hurts me down there, Mommy.
He does spank you a little hard, but he just wants you to be a good girl. I've got to go to work . . . .
Mommy, please don't leave me here. Please Mommy, please Mommy, please don't go . . . .

I spoke these heartbreaking words and documented them in my memoir, *From Sorrows to Sapphires*. In 2008, I founded Voice Today, a nonprofit organization whose mission is to break the silence and cycle of child sexual abuse and exploitation through awareness, prevention and healing to "Protect the Innocence of Children and Help Survivors Heal." It is an endeavor of the heart that arose from my own personal journey—the pain I experienced as a victim of sexual abuse, my triumph over shame, and my efforts to become empowered, to find value and worth in my life and help others do the same.

Since the age of three, I endured a living nightmare of physical and sexual abuse at the hand of my stepfather. At age 17, with no intervention, I desperately wanted an escape and attempted to take my own life. But, God had other plans for me, and through His divine intervention my life was spared. I stand today victorious as a loving wife, a devoted mother, and a successful professional. The Lord helped me claim victory over my past and turned my pain into a platform to help others heal.

My intimate knowledge of the trauma of child physical, emotional and sexual abuse has led me to become a leading activist in protecting the next generation of children. Together, we must address this issue with transparency, courage and action. Many are not aware of this epidemic that impacts one in four girls and one in six boys who are sexually abused before their 18th birthdays. Even more heartbreaking, only one in ten children will ever tell.

Tragically, 93% of abuse is perpetrated by someone the child knows, loves and trusts—perpetrators who are often within the family or extended family. Children become compliant in their abuse because they have no voice. Silence becomes their answer to avoid harm, or threats of harm, from those they love. They not only live in silence, but also in constant fear and endless shame. The psycho-emotional effects are as long-lasting as they are devastating.

Voice Today supports healing for survivors by hosting annual retreats for both youth and adults each fall as well as survivor support groups and healing workshops. As a crusader, activist and child advocate, I launched the Voice Movement campaign in the national media to ensure that the epidemic of child sexual abuse remains an integral and important part of the public consciousness. In April 2014, I also established White Out Child Sexual Abuse Day to be commemorated every April 30 during national Child Abuse Awareness Month. To learn more about these initiatives, I encourage you to visit www.voicetoday.org.

The impact of abuse on our children is a lifetime sentence, murdering their innocence, self-worth, trust and ability to achieve. In my life, I know all too well that my worth comes from the redeeming and restorative power of God, turning my pain into passion and my mess into a message through the mission of Voice Today.

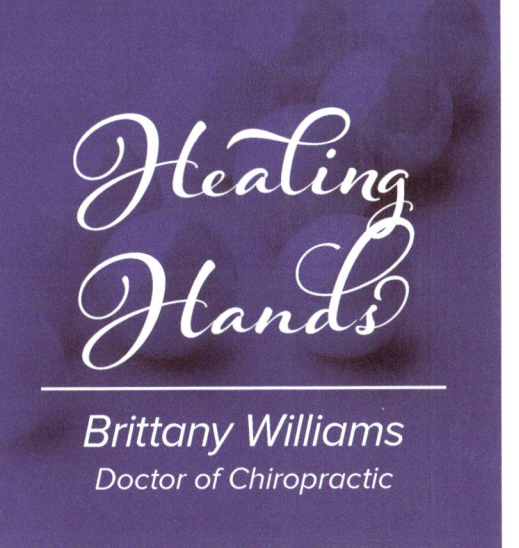

Healing Hands

Brittany Williams
Doctor of Chiropractic

Webster defines worth in one form as "having a value of," or "equal in value to." I like to think it should be defined as "what value you give." My father always has been a man of many values, many talents, and many things that, for me, set him apart not only from every other man, but also from every other person I have ever met. He is the type of person who would give you the shirt off his back or the shoes off his feet, regardless of what you've ever done to him, for no reason other than it was the right thing to do.

Among all these things, he's served in the military, been an All-Star athlete, and been married to his high school sweetheart more than 30 years. He owns cows, is the ultimate "Mr. Fix-it," and alongside his father built a four-bedroom home for his wife and children from the ground up. I couldn't have picked a better hero if I hand picked him myself. Of all my many blessings, I like to think he is one of the greatest fathers ever bestowed.

In 2009 at a family gathering, my father fell. Sounds simple, right? This fall extended his spine to the point that it was severed. Instantly, he lost all feeling below his neck. My mother rushed him to the emergency room. The doctor on call, a neurologist, examined this man with no feeling below his neck and decided he should go home. He assumed my father was drunk and that he should be discharged. My mother stayed and insisted my father be given a second exam and, then, a third. Finally, they determined he had a spinal cord injury and should be rushed to a nearby city for spinal surgery. He spent months at a nationally renowned hospital in Atlanta, Georgia, devoted to the medical treatment, research and rehabilitation of people with spinal cord injuries.

That year was my very first year at Life University. There, I found a group of people that believed we live in a world that only addresses symptoms instead of the true sources of our illnesses or injuries. I decided that chiropractic practice is what I want to do with the rest of my life. This is the value I give to the world. This is my worth.

I could have, and would have, lost my father that day in January 2009; the section of his spinal cord that was partially severed controlled his breathing. We learned later he had a herniated disc that was causing him to limp and, in turn, caused him to trip and fall. He had gone to many doctors—all of them gave him muscle relaxers and, not once, analyzed him in any detail.

I completed my degree, and I am now in practice. My worth is the drive I bring to this world as a doctor who knows how important it is to take that second, third, fourth look. I am a doctor who also knows that God's design is perfect; as long as we respect it, nurture it, and take care of health problems that arise, we will function as He intends us to function.

My father is still under chiropractic care in our hometown. We can now add driving back to his many talents, because he started doing that again two years ago. Pretty good for a guy they said would never walk again, huh?

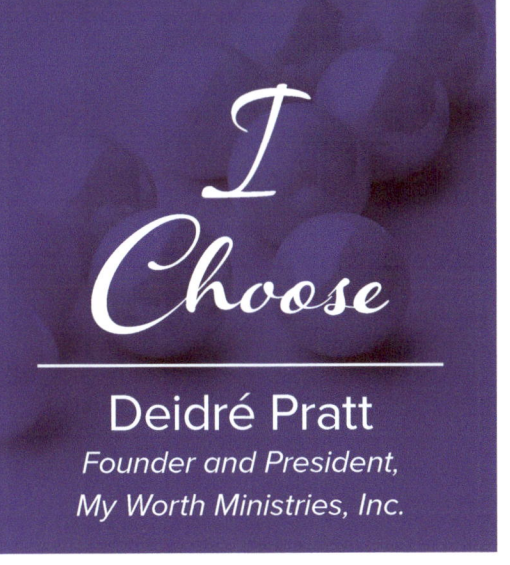

I Choose

Deidré Pratt
*Founder and President,
My Worth Ministries, Inc.*

This moment, I choose to be happy.

I choose victory over defeat.

This moment, I choose growth over unevenness.

I choose stillness over haste.

I choose a life full of truth.

This moment, I choose acceptance and realism over denial and fantasy.

I am choosing to be my very best friend . . .

This moment, I choose to

Honor

Forgive

Embrace

a being so dear that the hairs are numbered.

Yes, I am choosing to love me . . .

Today, Right Now, This Moment, and Forever

I choose me!

Copyright © 2005

Epilogue

Nothing Wasted.

No-thing wasted.
I need you to know there is not one single thing you've experienced in your life, or you're experiencing right now, that does not have a purpose. There is not one single thing in your life that will not be aligned and synthesized for a greater good—for something beyond yourself. I need you to trust that although you may not see the workings behind the scenes, there is a master plan in motion.

<u>No</u> thing—birth of a child, sexual abuse, broken home, honor student, first job, marriage, new home, domestic violence, divorce, rape, opening a new business, death of a loved one, nervous breakdown, new career, ministry collapse, athletic scholarship, academic scholarship, friends walk away, new friends come into your life, molestation, heartbreak, sickness, indiscretion, abandonment, new city, layoff, loss of home, they lied, she cheated, won the race, got voted into office, got voted out of office, financial downfall, father was not there, mother didn't care, struggling with identity, new position, new life—when I say <u>no</u> thing, I mean no thing, shall be wasted!

It all has a divine purpose. It is the good, the joys, the challenges, the painful, and the odious things we experience, whether revealed in a single defining moment, or represented in the series of these moments that will work together for our good. God has a master plan for your life. God designed you with "a hope" in mind. God chose you and revealed Himself in you. God has your future planned. And, know it is a really good plan. God did it for me, and I know He will do it for you.

God will give you the strength and the grace to:

- Let go; just simply let go.
- Make peace with your past.
- Forgive the process.
- Rise above adversity.
- Focus on your great future.
- Experience continual joy in Him.

Dear Heavenly Father,
Thank you for revealing my worth to me, and for choosing me to teach others how much they are worth. Amen.

WORTH Emerging Women Leaders STEM Scholarship Award

Science, technology, engineering and math—STEM—are fundamental. STEM education shapes the nation and will continue to contour the future of our country. The reality is that our nation's capacity to maintain a competitive position of global leadership rests on our ability to nurture future leaders—critical thinkers, out-of-the-box thinkers, end-to-end process improvement thinkers—who are poised, confident, and articulate innovators.

Studies have shown and time has proven that most jobs of the future will require a fundamental understanding of math and science. How do we stack up today? In comparison to students around the globe in places such as Singapore, Korea, Hungary, Australia and the Netherlands, the science aptitude of U.S. students is flat. America is falling behind internationally, ranking 25th in mathematics and 17th in science among industrialized nations. Other studies dim the light on our progression as a country to keep pace with the educational rigor of our children's peers throughout the world.

We know the projections:

- 7 of the 10 fastest growing occupations over the next decade will be in STEM fields
- 60% of the highest paying jobs within the last 5 years required STEM preparation
- STEM related fields pay 25% more than non-related fields

With a mere 16% of American high school seniors proficient in math, we have a lot of catching up to do. But, we can do it! I applaud the STEM-missioned programs and agencies forming across the nation. It's the right thing to do—to create the educational doorways to move us from mediocre to great.

My Worth Ministries, Inc. is ardent in its pursuit of advancing STEM education. We strive to be a doorway to relevant education. We also recognize that a well-rounded, STEM-based education is not only essential for future careers, but also essential to ensuring that our future leaders have a sound foundation of their identities and their worth.

The fusion of forward-driven STEM education and the healthy development of individual worth brightly color the future of our students, enabling them to cultivate the ability to lead both effectively and balanced. This is at the heart of educational leadership. This is at the heart of My Worth Ministries' education platform.

Unite with Worth . . .

My Worth Ministries has established a college scholarship program in support of young women pursuing college careers in STEM majors. Each year, outstanding students will be selected through a nationwide competitive application process to be the recipient of the WORTH Emerging Women Leaders STEM Scholarship Award. We encourage you to support this initiative by making a tax-deductible contribution to this worthwhile scholarship fund. Contributions may be made online at **www.myworthministries.com** or by personal check, payable to WORTH STEM Scholarship Award, and mailed to:

WORTH STEM Scholarship Award
P.O. Box 391744
Snellville, Georgia 30039

Thank you for your generous support of our mission to change the world and the trajectory of the lives of women—one young woman at a time. To learn more about My Worth Ministries and the WORTH Emerging Women Leaders STEM Scholarship Award, we invite you to visit our website at www.myworthministries.com.

Acknowledgements and Credits

"What God intended for you goes far beyond anything you can imagine."
– Oprah Winfrey

To the brave and beautiful women who shared their journeys as part of this collection, you are God's leading ladies! Your voices now echo by sharing with others your stories of worth. Thank you for journeying with me and for your resounding encouragement along the way.

Pastor Jesse Curney III, Senior Pastor, New Mercies Christian Church, Lilburn, Georgia: For more than a decade, you have been and continue to be my spiritual father, no matter where God's path for my life directs me. I am forever grateful that God used you to allow my broken wings to heal and for inspiring me to "totally yield" to God's voice and His plan for me. Your encouragement, advice, prayers, and covering uplift me. Thank you for believing in me, and may God bless you and First Lady Aleana, always.

When God places the right people in your life, the right things happen. Denise McFall, God placed you on this project with me and the right thing happened. Thank you for your commitment to *Worth*. Most of all, thank you for your inspiration and coaching as you help me achieve my dreams.

Regina Gibbs, you always have made it known that I matter to you and that you believe in the call on my life. I appreciate all that you have done to make *Worth* a reality. Love you, Mama Regina.

More than a friend, Tyra Williams, you are a sister to me—my confidante, my steadfast supporter.

To my parents, Ellerton Pratt and Doreen Priscilla Brown, through you God birthed a daughter of the Kingdom of God who lives a life knowing every day that she is worth it.

Grandmother Doris Brown, at 94 years old you remain remarkably brilliant. I recall the morning of your 93rd birthday when you shared with me on the phone that as you awoke and thanked God for life, you asked God if He was satisfied with you . . . because your soul was ready to do even more. Thank you for letting your light shine for all of these years. I love you, Grammy.

To my brother, Kirkland Pratt, when we were kids, it was always just the two of us, "Kirk and Dee," paired as if twins. I always knew that you would be there. And, no matter the winds of life, that's exactly where you've been. You always knew that I was worth it!

Bishop Dale C. Bronner, under your anointing and prophetic pastorship at Word of Faith Family Worship Cathedral, my capacity has expanded in so many areas of my life. . . Indescribable. Thank you. . . May God bless you and Dr. Nina.

Lastly, to my dearest son, Cameron: God trusted me with the most powerful, most inspiring, most brilliant and loving son. You give me a reason, daily, to never give up. I am the one who is supposed instill in you your value and worth; yet, you are the one who tells me every day, in both word and deed, how much I am worth. I love you dearly.

– Deidré

A heartfelt thank you to the amazingly talented and committed *Worth* production team:

>Denise McFall, Editor/Production Coordinator
>Lakia Ross, Graphic Designer
>Tammy McGarity, Photographer
>Alicia Igess - Urban Tangles, Hair Stylist
>Nyssa Green - The Green Room Agency, Makeup Artist
>Courtney Gower, Makeup Artist Assistant

www.ingramcontent.com/pod-product-compliance
Lightning Source LLC
Chambersburg PA
CBHW042348300426
44110CB00032B/61